D

Fact Finders™

Biographies

Francisco
PIZARRO

by Thomas Streissguth

Consultant:

John P. Boubel, Ph.D.
History Professor, Bethany Lutheran College
Mankato, Minnesota

Capstone *press*

Mankato, Minnesota

Fact Finders is published by Capstone Press
151 Good Counsel Drive, P.O. Box 669, Mankato, Minnesota 56002
www.capstonepress.com

Library of Congress Cataloging-in-Publication Data
Streissguth, Thomas, 1958–
    Francisco Pizarro / by Thomas Streissguth.
    p. cm.—(Fact finders. Biographies)
    Summary: An introduction to the life of sixteenth-century Spanish explorer Francisco
Pizarro, who conquered Peru while seeking a land filled with gold, silver, and other riches.
    Includes bibliographical references and index.
    ISBN-13: 978-0-7368-2488-0 (hardcover)
    ISBN-10: 0-7368-2488-X (hardcover)
    1. Pizarro, Francisco, ca. 1475–1541—Juvenile literature. 2. Peru—History—Conquest,
1522–1548—Juvenile literature. 3. South America—Discovery and exploration—Spanish—
Juvenile literature. 4. Explorers—South America—Biography—Juvenile literature.
5. Explorers—Spain—Biography—Juvenile literature. [1. Pizarro, Francisco, ca. 1475–1541.
2. Peru—History—Conquest, 1522–1548. 3. South America—Discovery and exploration—
Spanish. 4. Explorers.] I. Title. II. Series.
F3442.P776S77 2004
985'.02'092—dc22   2003015256

Editorial Credits
Roberta Schmidt, editor; Juliette Peters, designer; Linda Clavel and Heather Kindseth,
    illustrators; Deirdre Barton and Wanda Winch, photo researchers; Eric Kudalis,
    product planning editor

Photo Credits
Art Resource, NY/The New York Public Library, 11; Werner Forman, 16
Corbis/Vanni Archive, 6–7
Getty Images/Hulton Archive, cover
Library of Congress, 19
Mary Evans Picture Library, 12–13, 14–15
North Wind Picture Archives, 1, 4–5, 9, 10, 17, 22, 23, 25
Stock Montage Inc., 20, 21

Table of Contents

Chapter 1

Crossing the Line

The tall man pulled out his sword. He used it to draw a line in the dirt. He looked at the men in front of him.

He told the men that on one side of the line was an easy life of comfort. On the other side was a hard life of hunger and danger. Panama was on one side. The land of gold was on the other side. The men had to choose between comfort and adventure.

Francisco Pizarro and his men were on an island near South America. The year was 1527. Pizarro already had led them through many hard times. They had marched through swamps and deserts, rain and heat. Now they were almost out of food and water.

Pizarro dared his men to follow him to the land of gold.

Pizarro was more than 50 years old. But he was not ready to give up. He was sure they would find the land of gold.

Thirteen men crossed the line to join Pizarro. They would **conquer** Peru.

Chapter 2

A Spanish Beginning

Francisco Pizarro was born in Trujillo, Spain. He was born sometime between 1470 and 1475. Pizarro's parents were Gonzalo Pizarro and Francisca González.

As a child, Pizarro did not go to school. He never learned to read or write. Pizarro took care of pigs when he was young. When he got older, he joined the Spanish army.

Pizarro left Spain in 1502. He wanted to be rich and famous. He decided to go to the lands that Christopher Columbus had found 10 years earlier. Pizarro was sure he could find riches in that "New World."

A statue of Pizarro on a horse stands in Trujillo, Spain.

Chapter 3

The New World

Pizarro did many things in the New World. He lived on the island of Hispaniola for a few years. In 1509, Pizarro joined a group of men who **explored** Central and South America. In 1513, he joined an **expedition** led by Vasco Núñez de Balboa. Three weeks later, Pizarro became one of the first Europeans to see the Pacific Ocean. In 1519, Pizarro helped start the **colony** of Panama.

Pizarro could have lived comfortably in Panama for the rest of his life. He owned land and slaves. But he was not happy. He still wanted to be rich and famous.

In 1513, Vasco Núñez de Balboa led the first European expedition to the Pacific Ocean.

▲ Hernán Cortés conquered
the Aztec Indians in Mexico.

The Urge to Explore

Pizarro heard stories about other men in the New World. These men were exploring unknown lands. Some were finding riches and becoming famous. One such man was Hernán Cortés. Pizarro heard how Cortés conquered the Aztec Indians in New Spain. New Spain is now Mexico.

Pizarro also had heard stories about a land far to the south. This land became known as Peru. Indians said this land was filled with gold, silver, and other riches. Pizarro decided that going to Peru was his chance to become rich and famous.

The Partners

Pizarro needed help to get to Peru. Diego de Almagro and Father Hernando de Luque became his partners. Almagro helped Pizarro get men, ships, and supplies. Father Luque helped him get permission from the **governor** of Panama to go to Peru.

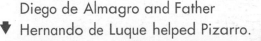

Diego de Almagro and Father Hernando de Luque helped Pizarro.

Chapter 4

The Land of Gold

Pizarro's first expedition to Peru started in November 1524. Pizarro left Panama with one ship and about 100 men. They sailed south to what is now Colombia.

Pizarro and his men searched for the land of gold for many months. They found swamps, alligators, and snakes. They did not find much gold. Pizarro and the men returned to Panama.

Pizarro, Almagro, and Father Luque did not give up. They planned another expedition. They got more money, more men, and more supplies.

This image shows Pizarro and his men leaving on the first expedition with three ships. They actually had only one ship.

Looking for Gold

In 1526, Pizarro left Panama on his second expedition. This time he had two ships, 160 men, and a few horses.

Pizarro and his men traveled farther south than before. They found more Indians and more gold. They also heard stories about a great city in the mountains. The gold came from that city.

After a few months of exploring, the group split up. Pizarro and a handful of men stayed on the island of Gallo. Almagro, the ships, and the rest of the men went back to Panama to get more supplies.

FACT!

Almagro battled with some Indians during the first expedition. He was hit in the face and lost one of his eyes.

▲ This 1530s image shows what some Peruvian Indians looked like when Pizarro met them.

Costly Expeditions

Back in Panama, the governor did not care about the gold Almagro showed him. The governor did not want to help Pizarro anymore. Pizarro's expeditions cost too much money. The governor sent two ships to take Pizarro and his men back to Panama.

When the ships got to the island, Pizarro did not get on board. He dared his men to stay with him. Thirteen men crossed the line and stayed.

Seven months later, Almagro returned to the island with one small ship. Pizarro and the men got on board. They sailed south.

▲ The Incas made this bird from gold between 1400 and 1534.

The Inca Empire

In 1527, Pizarro reached the Indian village of Tumbes. Pizarro found plenty of gold in Tumbes. He also learned that Tumbes was not just a small village. It was part of the great Inca **Empire**.

Pizarro spent many months sailing farther south and learning about the Inca Empire. The Inca Empire covered a large area in South America. One man ruled over all the land and people. But most important to Pizarro, the Inca Empire had a lot of gold and silver. Pizarro wanted to conquer this rich land for Spain.

Asking for Help

Pizarro returned to Panama. He told the governor he had found the land of gold. Pizarro wanted to **claim** it for Spain. He asked the governor for help. The governor said no.

Pizarro decided to ask the king of Spain for help. Pizarro reached Spain in 1528. He told King Charles about Peru. The king agreed to Pizarro's plan.

Pizarro asked King Charles for help to ▼ conquer Peru.

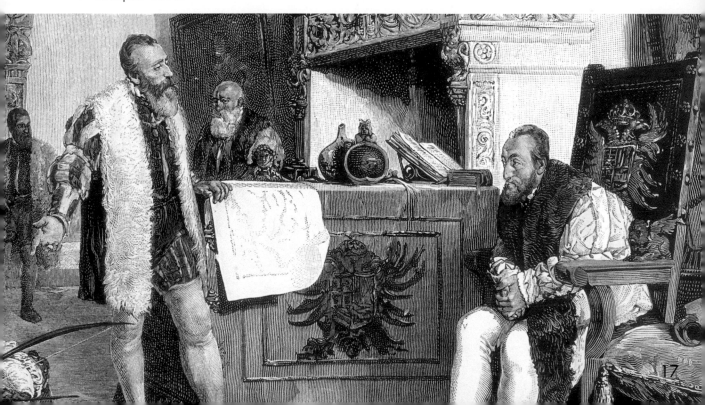

17

Chapter 5

The Conquest

In January 1531, Pizarro once again left Panama for Peru. He had three ships and 180 men with him. Almagro stayed in Panama to get more men and supplies.

Pizarro started his conquest north of Tumbes. At first, the Incas did not know that Pizarro wanted to conquer them. They soon learned the truth. Pizarro and his men took food, gold, and anything else they wanted.

The Spanish fought with the Incas. The Spanish had guns. The Incas had bows and arrows.

▲ Atahualpa defeated his brother Huascar and became the emperor of the Incas.

Timing

Pizarro had chosen a good time for his conquest. The Inca Empire was weak. Many Incas had died during the war between Huascar and Atahualpa. These brothers were fighting over who should be the **emperor**. Many other Incas died from **diseases** that the European explorers unknowingly brought from Europe.

Pizarro had another advantage. The Incas were afraid of guns and horses. They had never seen guns or horses before.

By September 1532, Pizarro felt ready to meet Atahualpa, the emperor of the Incas. Pizarro planned to make Atahualpa his **prisoner**. Pizarro could then conquer the Inca Empire more easily. He and about 200 men set off to meet the emperor in the city of Cajamarca.

The march from the coast to Cajamarca was long and difficult. The roads through the mountains were steep and narrow. Pizarro worried that the Incas would attack them. But Pizarro and his men arrived safely.

▲ Pizarro and his men followed winding paths and climbed steep hills to get to Cajamarca.

FACT!

On the way to Cajamarca, Pizarro and his men sometimes swam across rivers or used bridges made of vines and logs.

▲ Pizarro and Atahualpa met in the town of Cajamarca.

The Inca Emperor

Pizarro met Atahualpa in Cajamarca on November 16. Pizarro laid a trap for the Incas. Pizarro's men hid out of sight. At Pizarro's signal, they attacked the Incas. Atahualpa and his men did not have weapons. Pizarro's soldiers killed more than 2,000 Incas that day. Atahualpa was taken prisoner.

The Ransom

Atahualpa offered to fill a room with gold in return for his freedom. Pizarro agreed. But after the treasure arrived, Pizarro changed his mind. He was afraid Atahualpa would lead his army to attack the Spanish. Pizarro had the Inca emperor killed.

The Fall of the Empire

After conquering Cajamarca, Pizarro moved south to Cuzco, the Inca capital. Pizarro killed more Incas and took more gold. The Incas fought back, but they could not win. Pizarro took over Peru. The great Inca Empire ended.

▲ Atahualpa was sentenced to be burned to death. But because he agreed to become a Christian, he received the quicker death of being strangled.

FACT!

The room filled with gold was about 22 feet (7 meters) by 17 feet (5 meters). The gold was more than 8 feet (2 meters) deep.

23

Chapter 6

After the Conquest

Pizarro became the ruler of Peru. He built his capital city near the Pacific Ocean. He called the capital *El Ciudad de los Reyes*, or The City of the Kings. Today, this city is called Lima.

In 1537, war broke out between Almagro and Pizarro. Almagro felt Pizarro had cheated him out of money and land. He and his army took over the city of Cuzco. Pizarro sent an army to Cuzco. His army fought Almagro's army and won. Pizarro's men killed Almagro on July 8, 1538.

Almagro's friends did not forgive Pizarro. They attacked and killed Pizarro in his home on June 26, 1541.

Pizarro drew a cross in blood as he died. ➤

Lasting Impact

Peru became a base for more exploration. Many Spanish ships set out from Peru to explore the Pacific Ocean. Young explorers also went south to Chile and north to Ecuador. Their expeditions helped start these two countries.

Pizarro's conquest of Peru was one of the most important events in history. Peru changed Spain and Europe. The huge amounts of Inca gold made Spain one of the richest and most powerful countries in Europe. In return, Spain changed Peru and much of South America. The Spanish language and many Spanish customs became a part of South America's culture.

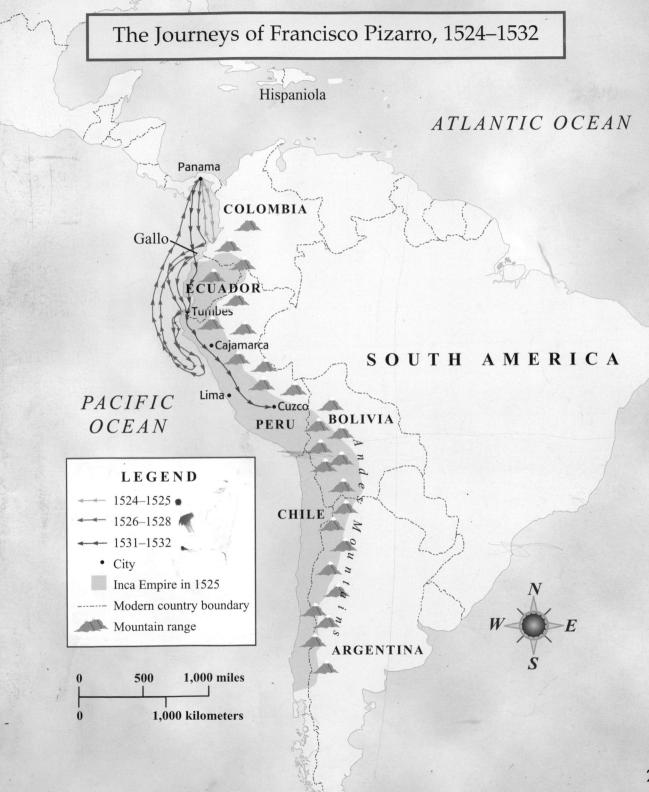

The Journeys of Francisco Pizarro, 1524–1532

Hispaniola

ATLANTIC OCEAN

Panama

COLOMBIA

Gallo

ECUADOR

Tumbes

• Cajamarca

SOUTH AMERICA

PACIFIC
OCEAN

Lima •

• Cuzco

PERU

BOLIVIA

CHILE

Andes Mountains

ARGENTINA

LEGEND

1524–1525 •

1526–1528

1531–1532

• City

Inca Empire in 1525

Modern country boundary

Mountain range

| 0 | 500 | 1,000 miles |

| 0 | 1,000 kilometers |

N
W   E
S

Fast Facts

- Pizarro grew up in western Spain.

- Pizarro went to the New World in 1502.

- Pizarro was with Vasco Núñez de Balboa in 1513 when they became some of the first Europeans to see the Pacific Ocean.

- Pizarro led expeditions to Peru in 1524, 1526, and 1531. He wanted to find gold and claim land for Spain.

- Pizarro captured the Inca emperor and conquered the Inca Empire. He claimed Peru for Spain.

- Pizarro had his partner Almagro killed in 1538. In return, Almagro's friends and family killed Pizarro in 1541.

Time Line

Francisco Pizarro is born in Trujillo, Spain, between 1470 and 1475.

Pizarro is killed on June 26.

Pizarro accompanies Vasco Núñez de Balboa in the first Spanish expedition to reach the Pacific Ocean.

Pizarro conquers the Incas and wins Peru for Spain.

1470   1492   1507   1513   1519–1521   1522   1531–1534   1541

World Events

Christopher Columbus crosses the Atlantic Ocean.

Ferdinand Magellan's ship *Victoria* returns to Spain. It is the first ship to sail around the world.

The western continents are named after Amerigo Vespucci. They become known as North America and South America.

Hernán Cortés conquers the Aztecs and wins Mexico for Spain.

Glossary

claim (KLAYM)—to say that something belongs to you or that you have a right to have it

colony (KOL-uh-nee)—an area that has been settled by people from another country; a colony is ruled by another country.

conquer (KONG-kur)—to defeat and take control of an enemy

disease (duh-ZEEZ)—a sickness or illness

emperor (EM-pur-ur)—the male ruler of an empire

empire (EM-pire)—a large territory ruled by a powerful leader

expedition (ek-spuh-DISH-uhn)—a long journey for a certain purpose, such as exploring

explore (ek-SPLOR)—to travel to find out what a place is like

governor (GUHV-urn-ur)—a person who controls a country or state

prisoner (PRIZ-uhn-ur)—a person who is held by force

Internet Sites

FactHound offers a safe, fun way to find Internet sites related to this book. All of the sites on FactHound have been researched by our staff.

Here's how:
1. Visit *www.facthound.com*
2. Type in this special code **073682488X** for age-appropriate sites. Or enter a search word related to this book for a more general search.
3. Click on the **Fetch It** button.

FactHound will fetch the best sites for you!

Read More

Bergen, Lara Rice. *The Travels of Francisco Pizarro.* Explorers and Exploration. Austin, Texas: Steadwell Books, 2000.

Kline, Trish. *Francisco Pizarro.* Rourke Discovery Library. Vero Beach, Fla.: Rourke, 2003.

Manning, Ruth. *Francisco Pizarro.* Groundbreakers. Chicago: Heinemann Library, 2001.

Meltzer, Milton. *Francisco Pizarro: The Conquest of Peru.* Great Explorations. New York: Benchmark Books, 2003.

Index